Bugs

Skip Counting

Logan Avery

Ants work.

10

Grasshoppers jump.

30

Flies land.

Bees buzz.

50

Moths move.

60

Beetles crawl.

90

Fireflies glow.

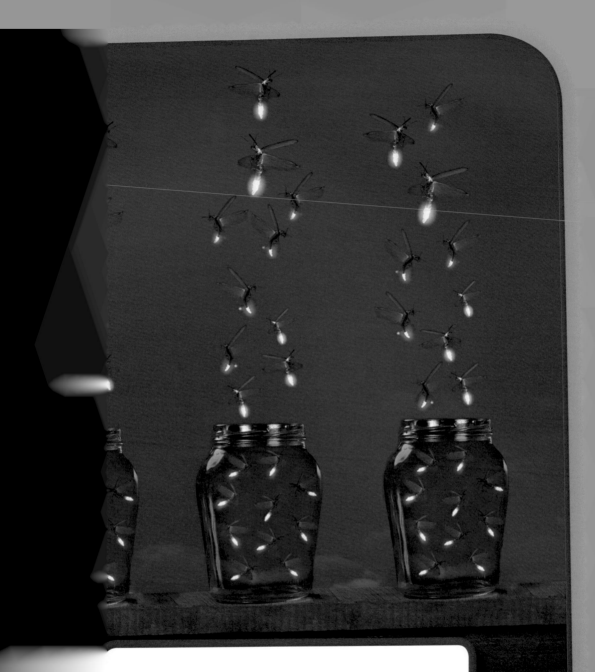

100

⚙ Problem Solving

Ladybugs are sitting on logs. Count the logs. Then, count the ladybugs by tens. Write numbers to complete the sentences.

1. There are _____ logs.

2. There are _____ ladybugs.

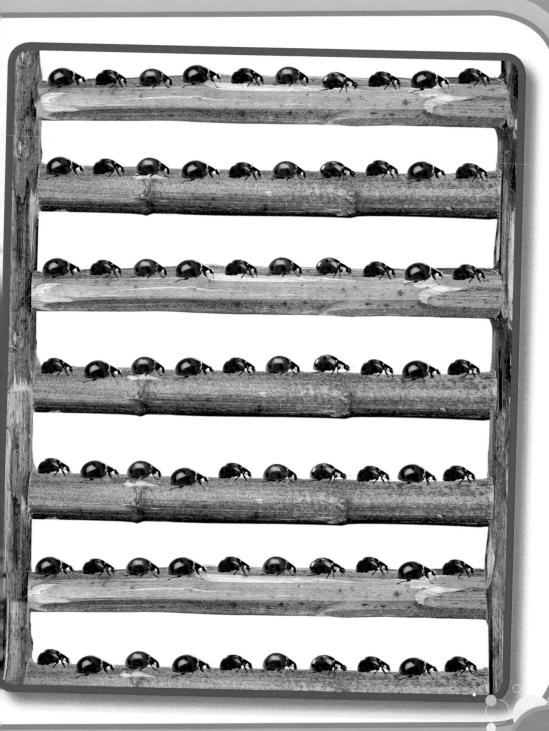

Answer Key

1. 7

2. 70

Consultants

Nicole Belasco, M.Ed.
Kindergarten Teacher, Colonial School District

Colleen Pollitt, M.A.Ed.
Math Support Teacher, Howard County Public Schools

Publishing Credits

Rachelle Cracchiolo, M.S.Ed., *Publisher*
Conni Medina, M.A.Ed., *Managing Editor*
Dona Herweck Rice, *Series Developer*
Emily R. Smith, M.A.Ed., *Series Developer*
Diana Kenney, M.A.Ed., NBCT, *Content Director*
June Kikuchi, *Content Director*
Véronique Bos, *Creative Director*
Robin Erickson, *Art Director*
Stacy Monsman, M.A., and Karen Malaska, M.Ed., *Editors*
Michelle Jovin, M.A., *Associate Editor*
Fabiola Sepulveda, *Graphic Designer*

Image Credits: All images from iStock and/or Shutterstock.

Library of Congress Cataloging-in-Publication Data

Names: Avery, Logan, author.
Title: Bugs / Logan Avery.
Description: Huntington Beach, CA : Teacher Created Materials, Inc., [2018] |
  Series: Amazing animals | Audience: K to grade 3.
Identifiers: LCCN 2017059899 (print) | LCCN 2018008539 (ebook) | ISBN
  9781480759510 (e-book) | ISBN 9781425856137 (pbk.)
Subjects: LCSH: Insects--Juvenile literature.
Classification: LCC QL467.2 (ebook) | LCC QL467.2 .A885 2018 (print) | DDC
  595.7--dc23
LC record available at https://lccn.loc.gov/2017059899

Teacher Created Materials
5301 Oceanus Drive
Huntington Beach, CA 92649-1030
www.tcmpub.com

ISBN 978-1-4258-5613-7